City Plot Perfect

Making Urban Spaces Thrive

Table of Contents

Chapter 1. Introduction

Welcome to our special report, "City Plot Perfect: Making Urban Spaces Thrive"! Get ready to embark on a lively journey through the vibrant world of urban planning and development. Our comprehensive coverage captures the heartbeat of modern cities, bursting with insights about how we nurture our most beloved urban spaces. From the lush green lungs to the pulsating squares and the bustling streets, every aspect of city life is intricately intertwined and masterfully shaped. Whether you're a city dweller longing for a bit of extra greenery, a keen city leader looking for inspiration, or simply a curious reader with an eye for the beauty of all things urban, this report has something special just for you! Prepare to be inspired and bring your urban space to life as we unravel the secrets of the city plots that are truly perfect. Grab your copy today - let's shape the future of our cities together!

Chapter 2. The Living City: Architecture and Urban Design

Urban planning and architecture are vibrant domains. They are marked by a constant symbiosis between the architects' inspiration and the pragmatic demands of a city's inhabitants. Encompassing smart urban design, eco-conscious practices, architectural wonders that define skylines, and the role of community collaboration, these studies form the lynchpins of our thriving urban spaces.

2.1. The Art and Science of Urban Design

Urban design bridges the gap between the built environment and social interaction, shaping both the physical layout of a city and the experiences of its inhabitants. It's an art where aesthetics and functionality coalesce - the essential components comprising thoroughfares, public spaces, and infrastructure.

In the study of any urban setting, it's vital to recognize the three core aspects: the cityscape itself (buildings, parks, roads, and other hard landscape elements), the interactions among denizens (social networks, economic system), and the transport system (buses, trams, cars, bikes). The ultimate design goal is to weave these facets into a harmonious whole that facilitates efficiency, promotes inclusivity, and enhances the quality of life.

2.2. Architecture: More Than Just Buildings

Architecture is the heart and soul of any city, creating visual masterpieces that define the skylines and form the backdrop for urban life. Engaging with architecture means seeing beyond mere concrete structures. Instead, it's the artistic embodiment of cultural identity, historical context, and technological advancements.

Cities endowed with beautifully designed buildings are naturally more attractive to residents and tourists alike. These structures inspire awe, serve as nurturing workspaces, provide living amenities, and promote communal interaction and creativity. The fusion of functionality and aesthetics in architecture illustrates how even the busiest city can be a space of tranquility and comfort.

2.3. Smart Urban Design: The Future is Now

The advent of technology has massively impacted urban design. Smart cities, espousing a new paradigm, integrate technology, urban planning, and citizens' participation guaranteeing a sustainable, efficient, and innovative living environment.

Smart urban design leverages the potential power of the Internet of Things (IoT), turning urban spaces into interconnected networks of devices. Technology-enhanced squares, parks, buildings, and transportation systems facilitate real-time data collection and analysis that inform the city management and drive smarter decisions. For instance, efficient energy management, AI-enhanced waste management, and smart traffic control systems are becoming integral to urban life.

2.4. Sustainable Practices in Architecture: Our Responsibility to the Earth

Sustainable architecture is shifting from niche to mainstream as cities increasingly face pressing environmental issues. Architects and urban planners aim to create structures and spaces that minimize environmental impact.

Eco-conscious architectural practices range from locally sourced materials to biophilic designs and renewable energy usage. Green buildings, green roofs, and vertical gardens are examples of architectural interventions that restore a balance between cities and nature, representing an antidote to prevalent urbanization-related concerns.

2.5. The Role of Community In Urban Design

City planning cannot be divorced from the people it serves. A people-centered approach lies at the heart of successful urban design. By involving local communities in planning and design processes, urban spaces become more inclusive and reflective of the inhabitants' needs and desires.

Residents' inputs into urban projects often yield spaces that are better integrated into the community fabric. This active collaboration nurtures a shared sense of ownership and accountability towards public spaces. By enabling public consultation and participation, cities not only become more livable but also gain a unique character that truly resonates with their residents.

In conclusion, urban design and architecture are not simply about fulfilling functional needs or adding aesthetic value. In the context of 'Living Cities', it's the collective soul of urban spaces, ecosystems, and communities, thriving towards sustainable, inclusive and participatory futures. It is both a technical and creative endeavor urging us all to understand and appreciate the essence of urban living - the vast, vibrant, evolving spectacle that it truly is. With technology, sustainability, and community participation as key drivers, the future of urban architecture and design is promising, pushing the potential of urban living to new exciting boundaries.

Chapter 3. Green is the New Grey: Parks and Green Spaces

The concrete jungle needs its moments of refreshment, and urban parks and green spaces play a pivotal role in this context. A verdant oasis amidst the grey metropolitan landscape, these green lungs act as sanctuaries for the city-dwellers — spaces to breathe, unwind, and connect with nature, amidst the relentless urban hustle. But the significance of parks exceeds far beyond aesthetic appeal and leisure. They serve essential ecological, social, and economic functions – platforms for community interaction, catalysts for biodiversity, and engines for property value.

3.1. Urban Green Spaces: A Multifaceted Elixir

To begin with, urban parks help mitigate some of the most detrimental environmental impacts of cities. The foliage acts as a natural air purifier — trees absorb carbon dioxide and other harmful emissions while releasing oxygen. The effect is a reduction in pollution levels and a boost to the overall air quality in city spaces. Additionally, trees work as urban heat sinks by soaking up the sun's heat during the daytime, increasing shade, and reducing surface temperatures and the heat island effect. Apart from these, parks and wetlands also work as water regulation systems. They absorb stormwater runoff and help recharge groundwater sources, mitigating flood risks and enhancing the city's resilience to climate change.

3.2. Parks as Breeding Grounds for Biodiversity

Parks are islands of biodiversity in the sea of concrete. They form a pitstop for migratory birds, and the various tree species attract an array of urban-adapted fauna. From squirrels and rabbits to butterflies and bees, urban parks brim with life, enriching the local ecosystem and offering educational opportunities about the natural world. Urban parks can mimic different types of natural habitats — grasslands, wetlands, woodlands — making them all the more important in conserving natural flora and fauna.

3.3. The Sociocultural Impact of Urban Green Spaces

From an economic perspective, well-maintained parks increase the property values of surrounding areas. They attract business investments due to the enhanced profitability tied to locations near green spaces.

Parks are sociocultural hubs where communities coalesce, fostering social cohesion. They encourage active and passive recreation — playing, jogging, picnicking, or simply reading a book under the shade of a tree. They're venues for celebrations, markets, concerts, and public gatherings — physical 'social media' of sorts.

Furthermore, parks establish a sense of place and cultural identity, displaying public art pieces and memorials, or being named after renowned local figures. They bear historical and cultural significance, creating emotional connections between the residents and the city.

3.4. Mental Health and Green Spaces

The psychological benefits of parks are extremely crucial, especially in a time where urban stress is a growing concern. Natural green spaces are therapeutic, reducing stress and anxiety. Studies link regular exposure to nature with improved mood, cognitive function, and overall mental well-being. The sensory stimuli in parks — the scent of blooming flowers, the rustling leaves, birds chirping — drive sensory relaxation and mental rejuvenation.

3.5. Urban Parks: The Design Perspective

Designing urban parks requires careful planning. An ideal park should be accessible, multifunctional, safe, comfortable, and visually stimulating. It should cater to people of all age-groups and backgrounds, with provisions for play areas, exercise zones, seating areas, and nature trails, all harmonized in an aesthetic layout.

Moreover, the design should ensure the continuity of the urban ecological network. It should promote native species, maintain an ecological balance, and serve as a conduit for wildlife movement. The aim is to mold green spaces into effective urban ecosystems while maximizing their recreational and psychological benefits.

3.6. The Revitalization of Urban Green Spaces

As cities evolve, so should their parks. Revitalizing green spaces involves restoring neglected or underutilized areas and transforming them into dynamic, functional, and resilient urban landscapes. Various innovative approaches have emerged, for instance, converting derelict industrial zones into public parks, a movement commonly known as 'industrial rebirth'. Another trend is the 'urban farms' movement, which not only promotes local produce but fosters community engagement in growing food.

A renewed focus on green spaces also involves integrating nature into the urban fabric more closely, through initiatives such as green roof systems and vertical gardens. These innovative methods make it possible for even compact, densely populated cities to enjoy the benefits of green spaces.

3.7. The Future of Urban Parks

In the light of climate change and rapid urbanization, parks will play an ever more important role in urban life. They will work at the forefront of our fight against global warming, mitigating its impacts, and enhancing resilience. Embracing nature-based solutions in urban planning will benefit cities and their inhabitants in countless ways. Therefore, planning, designing, managing, and revitalizing urban parks should be integral to our urban development strategies.

In conclusion, transforming 'grey to green' entails a comprehensive understanding of parks and a conscious effort to integrate them in our urban life. For cities to thrive, green spaces should not merely be a pretty backdrop, but an essential part of the urban matrix — an ally in bearing the weight of urban pressures. Green, indeed, is the new grey.

Chapter 4. City Beats: Transportation and Mobility

An urban space breathes at the rhythm of its transportation systems. In every city pulsating with life, you'll find an intricate network of veins and arteries - roads, railways, bike paths, pedestrian trails - all delicately designed to bring the city to life. From the early morning rush hour, through the silent hours of the night, efficient mobility is a key determinant of a city's health and vibrancy.

4.1. The Role of Public Transportation

Public transportation: the lifeblood of any thriving city. From the earliest days of trolley cars and horse-driven omnibuses, to the ultra-modern high-speed rail and electric buses of today, public transit has always had a key role in shaping urban life. It's more than just a way to get from point A to point B; it's a social equalizer, providing access to opportunities and making city life affordable and sustainable for its residents.

Drawing on data from various cities across the globe, public transportation's myriad advantages have been amply demonstrated. By reducing dependence on private vehicles, it helps cut down on traffic congestion and reduces city dwellers' carbon footprints. It contributes to increased physical activity levels and lowers lifestyle diseases. And perhaps most profoundly, it facilitates social integration by breaking barriers between different socio-economic groups.

4.2. The Challenges and Opportunities of Urban Mobility

As pivotal as transportation is for city life, it's not without its share of challenges. Urbanization trends are consistently pushing the limits of our transportation systems; growing populations, expanding city borders, and constantly evolving lifestyle demands keep transportation planners always on their toes. From solving the puzzle of last-mile connectivity, to ensuring an efficient inter-modal transit system, and keeping pace with technology advances and sustainability trends, urban transportation faces a multitude of complex problems that demand creative and strategic solutions.

Yet, within these challenges lie the opportunities. As our cities evolve, so too must our understanding and approach to transportation. Technology has fantastic potential to reshape urban mobility: mobile apps for real-time transit tracking, contactless payments, ride sharing, autonomous vehicles, electric mobility, and so much more. These advances promise to make our cities smarter, more efficient, and more responsive to their residents' needs.

4.3. Sustainable Modes: Walking and Cycling

There's perhaps no mode of transportation more sustainable than our own feet or a simple bicycle. Walking and cycling not only promote individual health and wellness, but also contribute significantly to a city's overall quality of life. They are forms of active transportation - they cost little to no money, produce zero emissions, need minimal infrastructure, and help cultivate a closer connection with the cityspace.

Developing a robust network of pedestrian sidewalks and cycling paths comes with several benefits. It aids in reducing traffic congestion, cutting down air and noise pollution, and contributing to mental health and well-being. In essence, prioritizing walking and cycling in city design allows us to create more human-centered urban spaces - a crucial stepping stone to true sustainability.

4.4. Urban Freight: The Overlooked Aspect of City Transportation

It's a familiar sight: a truck weaving its way through city streets, delivering everything from groceries to furniture, tools to toys. Urban freight is a key part of our everyday lives, yet it's often overlooked in transportation planning. Surveys suggest that the impact of freight on city traffic, air quality, and noise pollution can be significant, and hence demands strategic thought.

Green and intelligent freight systems, like cargo bikes, drones, and smart logistics, are becoming increasingly viable and are receiving growing attention from planners. Not only do they promise to enhance urban freight efficiency, but also to decrease its environmental and social impacts.

4.5. Future of Urban Transportation - Towards Smarter Cities

As the urban world continues to evolve, our perspective of what is possible with city transportation is rapidly changing. We now have a rare opportunity to steer our cities towards a smarter, more sustainable future.

Autonomous vehicles, smart mobility, Mobility as a Service (MaaS), integrated ticketing, real-time data, eco-friendly fuels, telecommuting – there is no dearth of innovations that can disrupt how we perceive and execute urban mobility. These tech revolutions are expected to make transportation more efficient, more inclusive, more integrated, and ultimately more sustainable.

Urban transportation is a symphony, a complex interplay of different elements that must work in harmony. It is an art and a science, a delicate balance of designing for equity, efficiency, and sustainability. And as the beat of our cities quickens, our transportation systems must not just keep pace but should also guide that rhythm, and in doing so, help us choreograph the dance of our city life.

Welcome to the journey of city transportation and mobility, where every twist and turn is a step towards creating thriving urban spaces, where every stop and start is an opportunity to make our cities more liveable. It's a pulsating, vibrant world – come, be a part of it.

Chapter 5. Nurturing Communities: Social Interactions and Urban Spaces

Communities are the lifeblood of cities, interweaving varied beliefs, abilities, and experiences into the urban fabric. These social networks not only animate public spaces but also significantly impact individual and communal well-being. Urban spaces—whether they are parks, markets, or streets—form the backdrop of such interactions. When designed with an awareness of their social function, these cities strive, providing vibrant, nurturing environments that facilitate meaningful relationships, improve human health, and promote biodiversity.

5.1. The Role of Urban Spaces in Fostering Social Ties

Urban spaces are vibrant arenas where community ties are fortified. These spaces provide the chance to relax, interact, and engage with fellow city dwellers, beyond the confines of closed quarters. Urban planning and the design of urban spaces play a significant part in determining how these areas are used and enjoyed, who feels welcomed in these spaces, and how they contribute to building community.

Walkable neighborhood layouts, for instance, favor social interaction. Several studies show that people living in pedestrian-friendly neighborhoods have more friends, better social support, and a stronger sense of belonging compared to those living in areas where cars dominate.

Public squares or markets also play an important role in fostering a sense of community. These spaces can function as social hubs—a place for festivals, local markets, or simply where people meet. The presence of street furniture such as benches can also encourage social interaction by inviting people to sit, relax, and spend time with others.

5.2. From Spaces to Places: Designing with a Sense of Belonging

For an urban space to nurture communities, it needs to transform from a mere 'space'—a physical entity, to a 'place'—a locale with emotional resonance. This sense of place can be particularly cultivated by involving the community in the design process and creating spaces that reflect their identities and needs.

Communities become deeply attached to spaces that reflect their shared experience and history. By involving the community in planning and design processes, we can ensure that urban spaces cater to the needs of the local people, reflect their identities, and consequently foster a sense of pride and belonging. This collaborative approach is described as 'Placemaking.'

In Placemaking, public spaces are seen not only as a canvas for the physical manifestation of daily life but also as a place for social engagement and a vessel for shared community experiences.

5.3. Green Urban Spaces and Community Well-being

Green space is another factor augmenting community well-being. Such areas encourage physical activities such as walking or running and offer a respite from the city's noise and fast pace. Moreover, nature-based solutions like urban forests, green roofs, and rain gardens can improve physical health by filtering air, reducing heat, and offering a calming milieu.

Equally important are the social benefits of green spaces. They serve as meeting points to connect with neighbors, encourage outdoor play among children, and offer venues for community events.

Urban community gardens likewise create opportunities for residents to participate jointly in cultivating plants, improving physical health, psychological well-being, and promoting social cohesion. Moreover, these spaces have the potential for communities to engage in local food production, promoting food security and self-reliance.

5.4. The Promise of Future Urban Spaces

How we socialize will dictate the planning and design of future urban spaces. As virtual interactions steadily rise, designers would need to create spaces that make in-person interactions attractive and convenient.

Simultaneously, addressing socioeconomic inequalities would be central to designing inclusive urban spaces. A city that nurtures communities must prioritize affordable and safe housing, accessible services, and green space, ensuring all urban dwellers have access to a thriving environment.

Inclusivity should be in our blueprint. Incorporating universal design principles increases accessibility and ease-of-use for everyone, including people with disabilities, older adults, and children.

Migration and demographic shifts also call for adaptable urban spaces that can cater to the needs of diverse communities and reflect the diversity of city dwellers in design and decision-making processes.

The future of urban spaces lies in their capacity to embrace these shifting realities and to continually evolve to accommodate the diverse and dynamic needs of their communities. By keeping the focus on community well-being at the heart of urban planning, we can ensure that our cities are not just buildings made of bricks and mortar, but living, thriving ecosystems that nurture and uplift their inhabitants - making our urban spaces truly perfect.

Designing for social interaction, community involvement in design processes, commitment to green spaces, and foresight about socio-technological trends will guide us in designing future urban spaces that are more than just physical spaces - they provide the setting for our stories and the backdrop for our memories. Let's build cities that aren't merely places you live in, but places that live in you!

Chapter 6. Resilient Urban Habitats: Climate Change and Sustainability

Understanding the complex relationship between climate change, urban development, and sustainability forms the crux of resilient urban habitats. It's a vast topic accumulating many aspects including reducing carbon footprints, embracing renewable energy, establishing climate-resilient infrastructure, promoting green spaces, and fostering biodiversity.

6.1. The Unassailable Link: Climate Change and Urban Development

As urban areas continue to sprawl, their impacts on climate change become unavoidable. Cities consume 78% of the world's energy, emit more than 60% of global carbon dioxide, with the urban built environment playing a substantial role. High energy consumption, waste generation, deforestation, and land degradation contribute to greenhouse gas emissions, exacerbating climate change impacts. Simultaneously, cities must brace to endure climate change repercussions such as rising temperatures, sea-level rise, intensified precipitation, and frequent extreme weather events.

6.2. Embracing Carbon Neutrality: Buildings and Transportation

To counteract this escalating problem, cities can strive towards carbon neutrality in two primary domains - buildings and transportation. Efficient buildings are pivotal for reducing a city's carbon footprint. Implementing stringent regulations for new constructions, insisting on high levels of thermal insulation, installing energy-efficient appliances, utilizing waste heat, and incorporating renewable energy systems like solar panels or wind turbines are practical solutions. Low-carbon materials such as recycled steel, eco-concrete, and green roofs can further mitigate the environmental burden.

In the realm of transportation, cities need to shift from fossil fuel-based vehicles to electric or hydrogen-powered ones, invest in effective public transportation systems, promote walking and cycling through dedicated infrastructure, and implement carpooling or bike-sharing schemes.

6.3. In the Grip of Renewable Energy

Renewable energy's significance in creating sustainable urban habitats cannot be overstated. It fosters energy independence, job creation, health improvements, and innovation. Cities can harness renewable energy sources, including solar, wind, geothermal, and hydropower, offering an environmentally friendly alternative to conventional energy sources. Municipalities can stimulate the green energy transition through policies encouraging renewable energy use and providing incentives for installation.

6.4. Building Climate Resilient Infrastructure

Climate-resilient infrastructure is designed to withstand the escalating impacts of climate change. These structures are sustainable, adaptable, and robust, capable of rebounding from climate-related shocks. This approach includes developing stormwater management systems that handle intensified downpours, erecting seawalls or dikes to mitigate sea-level rise, establishing urban heat island mitigation strategies like green roofs or shading structures, and building infrastructure that can withstand extreme weather events.

6.5. Fostering Green Spaces

Urban green spaces form the lungs of cities, acting as oasis within the urban expanse. They absorb carbon dioxide, filter pollutants, reduce urban heat islands, enhance local biodiversity, and provide vital recreational spaces for residents. We need to prioritize preserving existing spaces while integrating more green spaces into urban design, from communal gardens and green corridors to vertical gardens and green roofs.

6.6. The Importance of Urban Biodiversity

Sustaining biodiversity is a key facet of creating resilient urban habitats. Not only does it contribute to the health of the global ecosystem, but it also supports urban environments by reducing pollution, providing natural pest control, and enhancing residents' mental wellbeing. Policies promoting native plant species in urban landscaping, establishing urban wildlife corridors, and employing ecological design principles can foster urban biodiversity.

Understanding and implementing these strategies form the stepping stones to creating resilient urban habitats that not only withstand the impacts of climate change but also provide sustainable, livable spaces for all. Together, we can transform our cities, and the world as a whole, into a greener, healthier, and more resilient space for all of us — and for the numerous generations set to inherit it.

Chapter 7. High Above: Skyline and Vertical Urbanism

Every city is a living organism, continuously growing and evolving. Its skyline, a symbol of its glory and aspirations, undergoes a transformation as the city accommodates its increasing population and the demands of urbanisation. This urban metamorphosis often sees a shift towards vertical urbanism, a fascinating concept harmonizing functional design, architectural marvels, and sustainable practices.

7.1. The Concept: Skyscrapers and the Skyline

Skyscrapers are more than just tall buildings. They are clear indicators of a city's cultural, economic, and technological progress, pushing the limits of urban planning and architecture, taking innovation and creativity to an entirely new height.

Humans have always been captivated by the grandeur of tall structures. The first skyscraper, the Home Insurance Building in Chicago, was only ten stories high, but its daring height was a revolution in the architectural world. It was designed by William Le Baron Jenney in 1885 and used a metal frame previously unseen, allowing for lighter and taller construction, also referred to as 'vertical urbanism'.

Modern skyscrapers are much more than just height, they incorporate amenities, services, biophilic design, and technologically advanced systems, all while paying homage to the cities' cultural and historical heritage. Integrating the daily lives of inhabitants with architectural expression and practical utilization of vertical spaces helps form a city's unique skyline and offers character to its urban profile.

7.2. The Architectural Influence: Design in the Vertical

In the field of architecture, the design of skyscrapers borrows elements from various disciplines, resulting in structures that are aesthetically pleasing, eco-friendly, and functional. Indeed, in today's sustainable engineering ethos, skyscrapers are expected to contribute positively towards reducing the ecological footprint of urban living.

From the tapered shape of New York's legendary Empire State Building, designed by William F. Lamb and completed in 1931, to the twisting and turning Shanghai Tower, designed by architectural firm Gensler and completed in 2015, the evolution of skyscraper design amply demonstrates how architects have embraced vertical urbanism and sculpted city skylines across the world.

Skyscrapers create vertical connectivity, stacking homes, offices, leisure facilities, and sometimes entire ecological systems in their footprint. Take, for example, Singapore's vertical green spaces, which blend architecture with nature to combat urban heat, increase biodiversity, and enhance residents' well-being - a celebration of man-made wonders and natural beauty alike.

7.3. The Functionality: Living High Above

Living high above the ground is a unique experience. It offers tenants sweeping panoramas of the city, a tangible sense of living in the heart of the urban playground.

Each floor, each vertical space, is carefully designed to provide functionality and comfort. From state-of-the-art offices that inspire productivity and innovation, to residential spaces that incorporate amenities like indoor gardens, pools, gyms, and shopping centers — vertical urbanism fosters the optimum utilization of space while catering to diverse resident needs.

The sky doesn't only offer breathtaking views. It holds the key to maximizing potential living spaces in our increasingly packed cities, a new way to appreciate breathtaking panoramas and participate in city life from an unprecedented perspective.

7.4. The Future of Skyscrapers: Sustainability and Smart Design

The future of vertical urbanism is exciting. As we move towards more sustainable societies, skyscrapers have started to integrate energy-efficient systems like renewable power sources, water conservation technologies, waste management systems, and other smart building operations, all for reducing their carbon footprints.

We are also seeing a surge in mixed-use skyscrapers, where different categories of facilities—office, residential, retail—are strategically positioned within a single building to maximize efficiency, reduce commutes, and create a more cohesive urban fabric. For instance, Kuala Lumpur's iconic Petronas Twin Towers embraces mixed-use design, embodying a singular unit of residential, business, and leisure zones, each seamlessly interconnected.

Today's skyscrapers are no longer standalone edifices piercing the sky; they are sustainable, inclusive ecosystems where life thrives vertically, linking the city's inhabitants with its unique skyline, emblematic of the progress of human society.

From bricks and steel to glass and gardens, the transformation of the urban skyline via vertical urbanism stands as a testament to human endeavor, revolutionizing the conception of traditional cityscapes and forging an unparalleled vision of sustainable urban living, high above and into the clouds.

7.5. Conclusion: Vertical Dreams

Vertical urbanism embarks on a high-minded quest to combine the best aspects of urban living in a sustainable, efficient, and aesthetically pleasing format. This concept, although challenging, is an answer to many urban issues, providing solutions for overpopulation and land scarcity, as well as making cities more liveable, vibrant, and fully integrated.

The skyscrapers standing against the skyline, while depicting the city's aspiration, also mirror our dreams. Dreams of living in harmony with the environment, dreams of balanced societies, and dreams of exploring the limitless sky. These vertical dreams are a celebration of urban life, an ode to cityscapes, and a beacon of human achievement where the sky is no longer the limit, but the ultimate medium of expression.

With more cities globally adopting vertical urbanism, we continue to redefine the way urban spaces flourish, strut high, and yet remain deeply rooted to the grounds, embodying a contrast between the simplicity of human needs and the complexity of urban desires.

Chapter 8. Brick by Brick: Housing and Neighborhood Planning

The symphony of a city unfolds in its neighborhoods. The homes and the streets come together to create a melodious harmony that forms the rich tapestry of urban life. Each neighborhood has a unique character, and it is through careful planning of these neighborhoods, 'brick by brick,' that we can create vibrant, inclusive, and sustainable cities.

8.1. Grounding the Foundations

Urban housing is a pivotal aspect of city life. Cities are built on the foundations of houses which, in turn, forms neighborhoods. Therefore, comprehending the basic principles of housing, including its structure, design and distribution, is critical. Understanding the demographic needs, geographical constraints, and the interconnectedness of various urban aspects are the premises upon which successful housing policies are formulated.

But building homes goes beyond just stacking bricks together. It's about crafting spaces that foster community living while ensuring privacy. It's about designing homes that facilitate airflow and natural light without compromising on aesthetics. It's about creating dwellings that recognize and accommodate the differing needs of its residents, from singles living alone to families with young children, from seniors seeking safety and convenience to millennials valuing flexibility and connectivity.

8.2. Planning for Diversity

Neighborhood planning aims to celebrate diversity and inclusivity. A well-planned neighborhood has a composition of housing types catering to various income groups, family sizes, and lifestyles. This mix establishes vibrant neighborhoods teeming with life throughout the day, ensuring social interaction and security.

Diversity within neighborhoods also extends to housing style and design. Every building in a neighborhood should not mirror each other to create monotonous landscapes. Instead, architectural creativity and innovation should be encouraged to offer visually appealing and diverse cityscapes.

8.3. Transporting Life to Neighborhoods

Contrary to the traditional view, modern neighborhood planning sees transportation as a catalyst for development rather than a byproduct. Adequate and efficient transportation infrastructure adds an essential layer to neighborhood design.

The proximity of homes to employment centers, retail outlets, schools, and recreational spaces should be prioritized. This layout not only minimizes travel times and reduces vehicular emissions but also promotes walking and bicycling, leading to healthier lifestyles. The introduction of mass rapid transit systems and dedicated bicycle lanes are perfect examples of how transportation planning is woven into the fabric of neighborhoods.

8.4. Transforming Landscapes

As the cities expand, it is pivotal to ensure the redevelopment of dilapidated infrastructures and efficient utilization of lands. The concept of urban renewal comes into play here - an attempt to revitalize aging and decaying neighborhoods while preserving their historical context.

Urban renewal projects range from loft conversions in old factories and warehouses to the creation of mixed-use developments on brownfield sites. These strategies provide a new lease of life to obsolete assets while enhancing housing availability.

8.5. Connecting with Nature

Even amid the bricks and concrete, the essence of nature can pervade. Green spaces, involving parks, squares, or even small gardens, are of prime importance in any neighborhood plan. These not only provide visually appealing and calming ambiances but also offer venues for community interaction and recreational activities.

Additionally, low-impact development (LID) techniques such as green roofs and rain gardens can be integrated into individual homes, contributing to the sustainable management of rainwater and enhancing the overall microclimate of neighborhoods.

8.6. Building Resilient Neighborhoods

The rise of climate change and related challenges have necessitated the planning for resilient neighborhoods. This implies designing and constructing houses capable of withstanding varied stresses, whether it be rising floodwaters, intense heatwaves, or even climatic wear and tear. Incorporating climate-sensitive designs and materials in housing, and context-specific disaster risk reduction strategies are pivotal aspects of building resilient neighborhoods.

Urban planning indeed is a fascinating world, an intricate jigsaw where every piece, every brick counts. The poetry of a thriving city and vibrant urban spaces is penned in the careful planning and diligent execution of housing and neighborhood designs. As urban designers and city dwellers alike, our calling lies in fostering these spaces, brick by brick, into homes alive with warmth, neighborhoods buzzing with life, and cities dancing to the symphony of progress.

Chapter 9. Space for Everybody: Inclusive and Accessible Cities

Urban spaces are not merely physical domains where human life unfolds; they are also intricate mosaics of social, economic, and cultural interactions. To make urban spaces thrive, it is essential to weave inclusivity into the very fabric of city life. Across the world, forward-thinking cities are championing the cause of inclusive and accessible development, creating spaces that are welcoming to all, regardless of age, gender, ability, or social standing.

9.1. The Ethos of Inclusive Cities

Inclusive cities respect diversity and foster a sense of belonging for everyone. They champion accessibility, embodying a commitment to remove physical barriers and ensuring universal access to services and opportunities.

Inclusion involves making a conscious effort towards enhancing accessibility. A physically accessible city is one where movement is uninhibited, and everyone can navigate the urban fabric with ease. The city's infrastructure, from its buildings and public spaces to its transportation systems, are all designed to eliminate hurdles and ensure access to all.

For city planners, accessibility implies not just physical mobility, but also economic and societal inclusivity. This includes offering affordable housing, quality education, and gainful employment opportunities, encouraging a healthy mix of different income groups. Also, it means embracing diversity and providing spaces for people of various cultures, faiths, ethnicities, and life histories to thrive and participate fully in the city's life.

9.2. Universal Design: A Path to Accessibility

Universal design aims to create spaces that can be accessed, understood, and used by everyone, regardless of age, size, or disability. It accepts diversity as a norm and asserts that an inclusive approach benefits all to benefit from city life. For example, curb cuts originally designed to aid wheelchair users have also improved street access for people pushing strollers, cyclists, or with luggage.

When considering universal design, cities can re-evaluate their existing spaces, like parks, playgrounds, and public buildings, ensuring that everyone can easily use them. For instance, providing wide, uncluttered sidewalks that are free from physical obstructions, offering shaded places to rest, installing ramp access at entrances, and placing easy-to-read signage at regular intervals can all contribute to making public spaces more accessible.

9.3. Harnessing Technology for Inclusive Urban Living

Urban living is being remoulded by the rise of smart technologies. On the one hand, these advances can create barriers, especially for those who lack the skills or resources to use new technologies. On the other hand, however, they hold tremendous potential for more inclusive cities.

Smart technologies, like mobile apps that provide real-time transit information or IoT-based solutions for improved city services, can help enable more informed and inclusive decisions. For instance, navigation technologies with audio prompts can assist visually impaired people in their movements, and smart traffic management systems can help manage rush-hours effectively, enhancing accessibility for everyone.

Moreover, citizen participation platforms and mobile apps allow people to voice their opinions, concerns, or suggestions, fostering a sense of belonging and collective decision-making. These are pivotal mediums through which residents can partake in shaping their cities, ensuring that urban development is a truly inclusive process.

9.4. City Policies: Pioneering Inclusive Growth

Policies are at the heart of inclusive cities. They shape the direction of development, steer growth, and define the rules for city living. Therefore, they must explicitly prioritize inclusivity and demand that all urban infrastructures, services, and public spaces are accessible.

Many cities such as Vancouver and Vienna are pioneering inclusion-led urban policies. For example, Vienna's integrated approach to urban planning, "Gender Mainstreaming", considers gender as a component in city design, ensuring that both men and women's needs are met in the public domain. Vancouver's "Urban Aboriginal Peoples Study" is an initiative that actively involves the indigenous people in the city's developmental planning, catering to their unique needs and perspectives.

9.5. The Way Forward: Shaping Inclusive & Accessible Cities

The drive towards inclusive and accessible cities is an ongoing endeavor. It requires constant learning, rethinking existing norms, and encouraging fresh perspectives. Citizen engagement, universal design, smart technologies, and inclusive policies are key tools for urban planners. Yet, the most instrumental tool is a collective commitment towards inclusivity, where every stakeholder, from government agencies and civil society organizations to business houses and citizens, play their part.

Inclusive city planning cannot be a one-size-fits-all approach. It requires tailoring strategies to local contexts, engaging communities in planning processes, and reflecting the distinct wants and needs of various groups.

In conclusion, inclusive and accessible cities are ones that invite diversity, break down barriers and foster a sense of belonging. Designing these cities is an intricate endeavor, yet entirely possible with the right tools and approaches. Let's strive towards creating cities that are not simply about surviving but thriving, for each one of us, together.

Chapter 10. Local Vibes: Small Businesses and Local Economy

When we consider the life pulsating through the streets of an urban haven, an undeniable force driving this vibrant energy is the local businesses. These establishments act as the heart of our neighborhoods, contributing to both their economic vitality and their unique character. Local businesses give our municipalities color, culture, and identity.

10.1. The Local Economy: A Close Connection

Understanding local economy starts with getting to know the lay of the land. What is a local economy, and why does it matter, you may ask? The local economy can be described as the system of exchange between businesses, individuals, and institutions functioning within a specific geographic boundary, such as a town, city, or metro area. Local economies thrive through the collective efforts of small and medium-sized businesses, creating jobs, producing goods and services, fostering innovation, and contributing to growth and vitality.

The connection between local businesses and the local economy is symbiotic. Businesses thrive when the economy is robust, and the economy flourishes when businesses are prosperous. This, in turn, encourages more investment and further economic growth, promoting a cycle of prosperity, strengthening the health of both entities.

10.2. Small Businesses: The Engine of the Local Economy

Small businesses often serve as the engine that propels local economies forward. They provide unique and necessary products or services, create meaningful jobs, and help create a sense of community.

A research study by the Small Business Administration (SBA) in the U.S. revealed that small businesses account for 64 percent of net new jobs. Moreover, the Impact of the 'buy local' movement has been profound, as money spent at a local business returns three times more money to the local economy compared to the same amount spent at a corporate chain.

There is, therefore, an economic multiplier effect that comes from local businesses. This effect signifies the capability of an initial spending to recycle within the local economy, thus multiplying the amount of overall output generated.

Local businesses also tend to invest their earnings back into the area, uplifting the local economy and contributing towards the area's affluence. These activities often incorporate donating to local charities, sponsoring local events, and supporting local initiatives.

10.3. Building a Community Identity and Culture

An immeasurable value of local businesses lies in the distinctive identity and culture they provide to the community. These spaces become more than just places to buy or sell; they turn into essential social spots fostering community connections and reinforcing a sense of belonging. Bookshops that host local authors' events, cafes displaying local artwork, or bakeries donating to the local food bank

– these are the threads that weave together the social fabric of a community.

Local businesses also contribute to the character and individuality of neighborhoods. The architectural designs, the types of goods and services, the decoration, and even the type of advertising, all help forge a unique aesthetic that differentiates one town, city, or neighborhood from another.

10.4. The Role of Urban Planning

Urban planning plays a crucial role in carving spaces for local businesses and thereby intrinsically linking with the local economy growth. Urban planners should consider the importance of supporting small businesses when designing master plans for cities. Preserving and designating spaces for local businesses, creation of business-friendly policies, ensuring easy access to public transport, and encouraging pedestrian-friendly neighborhoods can boost local economies.

Local government bodies and city planners need to ensure that the infrastructure supports the development and sustainability of these businesses. This includes providing adequate commercial space at reasonable prices, ensuring essential services, accessibility, adequate parking, and the like.

10.5. The Challenges

However, it's essential also to touch upon the challenges faced by local businesses. Rising rents and real estate prices, competition from big corporations, and the proliferation of online shopping have all posed significant challenges for small businesses. Additionally, the COVID-19 pandemic has caused substantial financial strain on many such businesses.

Despite these obstacles, local businesses continue to be resilient, innovative, and tenacious, often finding new ways to navigate challenges. Policies at the local, regional, and national level can play an influential role in supporting these enterprises to ensure they continue to flourish and bolster local economies.

In conclusion, local businesses and economies are the cornerstone of our urban spaces. Their success cultivates a thriving community and, conversely, a vibrant community fuels the success of local businesses. The symbiosis between these two facets of city life is integral to creating city plots that are not only economically prosperous but also culturally rich and livable. Through supporting local businesses, we pave the path for better urban spaces that are sustainable, healthy, vibrant, and inclusive.

Chapter 11. The Future of Our Cities: Smart and Connected Urban Environment

Cities, while offering an abundance of opportunities, experiences, and connections, also face tremendous challenges such as traffic congestion, pollution, and inefficient use or lack of resources such as energy, water, and space. It is here where the undeniable need for Smart and Connected Urban Environments becomes evident.

11.1. A Smart Future

To transform our urban spaces, we must lean on technologies that can help our cities become smarter and more connected. This means leveraging the Internet of Things (IoT), artificial intelligence (AI), data analytics, and various digital applications to innovate the way we plan, build, manage, and experience our cities.

Artificial Intelligence and Machine Learning can be used to predict traffic flows, optimize public transportation schedules, and design dynamic pricing models for energy usage. We also see cities using IoT to monitor environmental indicators like air and water quality in real-time, or to track the usage and availability of public amenities such as parking spaces or bike-sharing stations.

11.2. Enhancing Mobility

One key area where smart technologies can make a tangible impact is in the realm of mobility. On-demand ride-sharing services, powered by sophisticated algorithms, such as Uber and Lyft have already redefined urban transportation. But smart technology doesn't stop at ride-sharing services. IoT and AI can be used to optimize traffic light timing, predict usage patterns of public transportation, and provide real-time updates to commuters, thus making urban mobility smoother, more efficient, and more flexible.

What's more, the implementation of autonomous vehicles (AVs) will further revolutionize urban mobility. By reducing human error, AVs promise to drastically decrease traffic fatalities. As well as minimizing the space cars need on the road for safety reasons, thereby alleviating traffic congestion. The widespread adoption of AVs could even change the urban landscape itself, with fewer parking slots required, space could be reclaimed for green areas, pedestrian zones, or more housing.

11.3. Intelligent Infrastructure

The infrastructure within our cities will also evolve as they become more connected and intelligent. For instance, smart grids are designed to collect and analyze data on energy usage in real-time, enabling more efficient allocation of resources and reducing energy wastage. Cities can also leverage IoT to enhance water management, using sensors to detect leaks, monitor water quality, and optimize irrigation.

The buildings themselves can also be smarter. Intelligent building systems can automate lighting, heating, ventilation, and air conditioning based on occupancy or time of day, thus improving energy efficiency while simultaneously enhancing comfort.

11.4. A Greener Urban Environment

Above all, the smart and connected urban environment holds significant potential in addressing environmental concerns. From smart waste management solutions that identify the most efficient collection routes to air quality sensors scattered throughout the city sending information for real-time monitoring, the possibilities for creating a sustainable city are enormous.

Smart city technology also has a critical role to play in facilitating the growth of green space within urban areas. For example, sensor-based irrigation systems can help maintain urban green spaces more efficiently, while data analytics can help city planners identify optimal locations for new green spaces based on various factors such as population density, existing urban heat islands, and pedestrian footfall patterns.

11.5. The Human Aspect

While the technological aspect of smart and connected urban environments is critically important, we must also not overlook the human aspect. The key goal of the smart city transformation is to improve the quality of life for its inhabitants.

To achieve this, city planners and tech developers must engage with local communities, embracing co-creation and citizen participation. Citizens can contribute useful on-the-ground insights that complement the data picked up by smart city technologies. Furthermore, by encouraging citizens to be part of the decision-making process, we can foster a sense of ownership and enhance the social sustainability of smart city initiatives.

11.6. The Transformation of Governance

Another essential aspect of smart cities is the transformation of governance. With a wealth of data available from multiple sources, city governments can make more informed policy decisions. This can lead to increased efficiency, transparency, and trust between city administrations and their constituents.

Advanced data analytics can also highlight disparities and pinpoint areas of need, allowing city administrations to allocate resources more equitably. As a result, this aids in addressing socioeconomic inequalities, promoting social inclusivity, and paving the way for truly holistic urban development.

In conclusion, the future of our cities cannot be fully realized without a smart and connected urban environment. By leveraging technology, we can address various urban challenges, boost the efficiency of city services, promote sustainability, enhance citizens' quality of life, and more. It's a vibrant and exciting future, but the journey there requires careful planning, collaboration, and a commitment to putting people at the heart of the transformations that lie ahead.

www.ingramcontent.com/pod-product-compliance
Lightning Source LLC
Chambersburg PA
CBHW071013260726

48661CB00007B/2935